Wild Brides

POEMS

ELMER HOLMES BOBST AWARD FOR EMERGING WRITERS

Established in 1983, the Elmer Holmes Bobst Awards in Arts and Letters are presented each year to individuals who have brought true distinction to the American literary scene. Recipients of the Awards include writers as varied as Toni Morrison, John Updike, Russell Baker, Flora Lewis, Edward Albee, Arthur Miller, Joyce Carol Oates, and James Merrill. The Awards were recently expanded to include categories devoted to emerging writers of poetry and fiction, and in 1991 the jurors selected winners in that category, Robert Schirmer for his story collection, *Living with Strangers*, and Laura Kasischke for her collection of poetry, *Wild Brides.*

LAURA KASISCHKE

Wild Brides

POEMS

NEW YORK UNIVERSITY PRESS
NEW YORK AND LONDON

Manufactured in the United States of America

Library of Congress Cataloging-in-Publication Data

Kasischke, Laura.
Wild brides : poems / Laura Kasischke.
p. cm.
Includes index.
ISBN 0-8147-4620-9 (alk. paper) — ISBN 0-8147-4621-7
I. Title.
PS3561.A6993W54 1992
811'.54—dc20 91-28800
CIP

p 10 9 8 7 6 5 4 3 2 1
New York University Press books are printed on acid-free paper,
and their binding materials are chosen for strength and durability.

For Pete Siers

CONTENTS

Part 3

Part 4

ACKNOWLEDGMENTS

Grateful acknowledgment is made to the following journals where many of these poems first appeared, sometimes in different versions: *The Bellingham Review, The Beloit Poetry Journal, Crab Creek Review, Cutbank, The Green Mountains Review, The Greensboro Review, Jacaranda Review, The Journal, Painted Bride Quarterly, Passages North Anthology, River City, Spoon River Quarterly* and a chapbook entitled "Brides, Wives, and Widows" published in 1990 by American Studies Press.

"Palm" and "The Driver's Lullaby" were first published in *Poetry*.

A grant from the Michigan Council for the Arts provided support for the writing of this book.

I would especially like to thank the Ragdale Foundation for a residency during which many of these poems were completed. In addition, gratitude is owed to the Arts Foundation of Michigan for two generous scholarships which gave me the time and encouragement to study writing.

Wild Brides

POEMS

Part One

This one you've held
and will hold all your life
though it cuts a bit at your thumb
like a single sliver of glass that glints
from a quarry of slate. You
will die someday, of course, slowly
not young, not old. And before you're forgotten
the neighbors will speak of you fondly.
Now close your hand tight
on this secret. Die
with this secret but no regrets. Remember
this is how the small survive, the way
the small have always survived.

PALM

I see you will live an ordinary life, perhaps
have children, perhaps marry
a kind but un-
remarkable man. There
is a simple journey that waits for you
(Niagara Falls? Yellowstone Park?) Go
on it. Make
the decisions you have to make: paint
the upstairs bathroom blue, move
to Wisconsin. It doesn't matter.
But here, here in this crease, this crease
like a scar at your thumb—here
I see something more.
The drapes in this room will be red
and torn. Close them. Let him
show you slowly to the bed. No
you'll say, it's daylight
and my simple husband trusts me.
Trust me—this
is your moment—the one
you'll remember (the hot breath
of the August breeze, the sun
white in the sky, the trickle of sweat
on his neck: it will turn to salt on your tongue).

The Chorus:

So you, Medea, wild with love
Set sail from your father's house.

TIMESPAN

It's no wider than the span of my arms.
As the camera pans further   and further
from me, this becomes smaller
and smaller   and smaller

until   I'm back in my mother's body, I'm
the coldness at the center
of that scalding body, I'm no more
than a chip of ice in her burning girlhood.

She is dressed in white for Scarlet Fever
and the doctors expect her to die, her blood
is sea water infused with fire   and I
am oblivion curled away in a cave

of red-hot flowers. Perhaps God
would like to spade over my grave   but
it's winter, the cold ceramic
of the wash bowl burns her cheek

and cold-blooded birds flash wings as white
as His beard by her window. It starts
to snow   snow   and snow until
if the snow were any deeper, it would be the sky.

A train screeches its brakes out there
where my grandmother is standing
in boots and her camel's hair coat, watching
her only child die. This

is as close as they'll let her get. It falls
on all of us there, the metal
ringing of train wheels, fresh
blood on those tracks   and timespan

spirals to the deeper circles
of our hells. My mother smolders
and my grandmother shakes the snow
like ashes from her hair, white

hospital paint peels around the windows.
So   what's a miracle? I
lurch out of the frozen ground then   full-
bloomed and red as a poison rose

and my mother turns to the steamy window
and smiles   at her own mother who can see
the red strings of shredded flesh
gorgeous between her daughter's gleaming teeth.

WILD BRIDES

I pulled back the sheets from the bed
on my wedding night to find
wild brides between them, sweat-
soaked and delirious. Until then I'd believed
my life would become
a balance beam
and I would try to walk it, forever,
like a wife. I was wrong.
The wild brides hadn't heard
what the one-armed priest had warned.
They still wanted to sleep late, drink
pink wine for breakfast. Even
the gold ring couldn't keep
the bus driver from refusing the fare.
He didn't want a handful of dimes.
And the butcher still
slipped himself in
with the wet steaks between
the wet pages of butcher paper.
I had planned to try.
But there they were
the first night already
in spectacular white. My husband kissed
my hot wrist, and I thought

of Herod's daughter-in-law
dancing in a sheet on her wedding night—
heart beating like a furious bird
netted in skin—so wild Herod told her
he'd give her anything she wanted
for a wedding gift in the world.
I want the Baptist's head
on a platter she said. My flaming fingers moved
over my husband's young neck
and I imagined her there,
her blood-red hands full of hair.

WOMAN KILLS SWEETHEART WITH BOWLING BALL

The moon is loose in the gutter tonight
and it rolls without kisses
or handprints between us   Its mouth
is an O of surprise

O Tonight the phantasma of love
climbs the stairs while we sleep   She
sags with exhaustion and booze
and pills   while her skin hangs heavy
and empty as hate
She floats so slow she floats
as if she is swimming through blood

> *Shhh Shhh* the lights are out
> and the little suspicion
> sleeps and dreams
> and whimpers in its crib
> Its tongue is ugly and blue

She climbs   She climbs
in silence and fury   spinning groggy
in darkness and wind   Look
her left hand bears for you sweetly

a gift of lightning
and lilies to please you   Though
O   tonight
in her right hand she   she
has invented gravity

SOLOMON GRUNDY

Born on Monday to mucous and blood
and the arms of a teenage mother
slippery with dread, under a moon that crept
with mushrooms in the dark
while the bloodsuckers sucked and clung
to the dead. The world
is as watery as a womb, he thought,
gurgling and murky with tears.

Baptized on Tuesday with water and weeping
on a day so damp the frogs were dripping
in ecstasy out of the trees
and the priest was singing, "I exorcise thee"
and the warm wet diaper chilled
to the burning and blazing of sleet
and the Mary of Misery with her bare white feet
pierced his bladder with her plaster stare
and Solomon Grundy shivered and screamed.

Married on Wednesday for fairer or fouler
because the milk was warm in her veins
and the meat was sweet on her limbs
and the church bells shrieked in the steeples
and the housefly slept in the feces.

And where they met he was bathed
by the smooth white tongues of their sheets.
There was peace for awhile and love and she said,
We have gone together now to a place
from which there is no return.
His pleasure uncurled in her like the mercy of sperm.

Took ill on Thursday in the summer shade
of a fever tree, and the priest screamed,
"I exorcise thee!" and the nurse burst in
with her purse full of pills
and a lock of his hair, and spittle
and toads. They bandaged him,
x-rayed him, amputated all
of his watery toes, and never gave up hope until
the last coin rolled from his pocket, and still
on Friday he was ill.

Solomon Grundy got worse on Friday
and the sun washed away in the rain
and a nun flapped past in the inky wind.
His wife gave up and went home
where she slid right down into the oily mud
slick with the tongue of the neighbor's son.
And Solomon Grundy, toeless and blind,
listened to soap operas all afternoon, and he cried.

On Saturday Solomon Grundy died
and the priest buzzed around his corpse like a fly
and his mother picked maggots out of his eye
and his wife wiped the flower dry that wept
for another between her thighs.
And the slugs and the nothing clung and sucked.

Embalmed and gutted and buried on Sunday
and that is the end of Solomon Grundy.

THE CYCLONE

When I am sixteen I think
I'm falling in love with a boy
who's learning to play the electric guitar.
Hour after hour
passes by in his basement
in the blur of noise he is doing.
I sit on an old couch
and stare at him
until I hear only
a flutter of motion around my head
like a hot, churning bath.
For a moment he stops
and my empty head howls
the lull of a train
racing around and around me
until I finally drop dazed
out of a windstorm, many years
ahead of myself. The world
is technicolor and turning
and suddenly I'm
the mother of the boy who is learning
to play the electric guitar.
It's beautiful, summer, Saturday outside
and he's been down there all day with a girl.

The strain of it, the endless crescendo,
the bedlam of music and motion
lifts the house
into air, explodes
the sonic boom of breaking
the barriers of sound,
the upward locomotion
of making dinner, making love, waking up
everyday after day after day, the rumbling
of a platform in the past
where I am sixteen
and waiting for a train
while down the street
an old, deaf woman
is planting cabbage behind a shed.

STAGE DIRECTIONS

The father and daughter look at each other
then stop, their gestures and expressions freeze.

The mother, who is ill, rocks
in her chair between them.

There are stacks of old newspapers in this room.
To go back and read them all
would be the same as this kind of suffering—
tragedy becomes mundane
when it's articulated—so
no one reads.

There's no point in dialogue now.
Sewage seeps into the streets at night
and the glowworms pulse there greenly.
Stage left: a shabby
colonial-style sofa.
Stage right: the television blinks.

The characters get older during these directions.
This is the Midwest.
Up the road the same cows stand
cow to cow on the dairy farm forever. No sound.

No motion but the steel milkers.

The cows are crippled with the standing
and the year after year and still
they gush their milk and mercury despite themselves
into blank suckling machines. The excess
trickles into puddles around them, sours
and softens their useless hooves.

And look, the fine dust of the Milky Way
settles on their backs.

It is the Midwest. The river
up the road swims
with one-eyed catfish and salmon
blooming tumors in the cold
chemical dark.
The father and daughter look at each other.

The mother, who is ill, wonders
why they've tortured one another
this long. Maybe
she'd even prefer death to this.

There's no point in dialogue now,
no real reason, even,
to raise the curtain on this scene.

CANDY, STRANGER

Turned sixteen and the satellites
spy down the sky's dark throat at her:

rich girl, rich girl
a rich man built
her hometown from a kit

Some girls are just born knowing
this world of matter
is full of shit   and by now
the other suburban girls
are locked away for the night

where the TV beams its big blue eye
clean as aluminum through our hearts   all-
knowing but totally cold, we need
to be Movie Stars
or let us die, we make
our easy vows
to God: this year, this year

we won't eat and fear
stuffs us up in our bedrooms
like freezers of meat, we know

there are men
with terrible gifts in the dark but she

walks on fearless through the field
that will be her elegy

The incest the drinking
and the drugs
have dared her to this sharp dark while
the same dead child feeling
she's always had hates
the birthday wind and the anorexic
star-song of suburban girls

And what was the last useless fact
we memorized together in school?
On Mars the sky
is always red So this
is the last mystery
that can be revealed to her

The rest of us talk about it

until we aren't teenagers anymore
and the telephone lines stretch tight
as female terror where

our voices shoot without our souls
electric over the earth across
the dark time planet
we don't understand and through
the red swirling dust of the one we do

GODMOTHER'S ADVICE

Sweetheart, the world
and everything in it
and the backward spinning forward
while the chips fall and the blue fruit
consumes us: All

will be later and nothing, too,
where the branches blacken the trees
like winter and winter then suddenly spring:
The men will be angry, and
the blood clots, and
the gallstones

but don't cry: Listen
to the hum and the drum for omens—
for everything happens when we
are just about to relax, and the pigs
are snoring swinely in their pails:

Try to stay alive until you die.
Some night you will find yourself
singing in your car
on a street far from where you live
and the radio's on, and your eyes are tired:

Suddenly the street is a river of ice
and you are spinning in both lanes and learning
these laws of physics:
All the trees grow in the path of the wind
for a reason, and a billiard ball will roll

at the exact speed of the ball
that hits it from behind: The click
and spin of balls in the dark
and a truck whirls to you
and the windshield will kiss you

and laughter, and clapping. Remember:
The world is vulgar and everything in it:
The sweet of the melon
and the meat pie steam of being alive.
You will be crying

for more of that: The clock
will rant in the waiting room
while the pallbearer stumbles in his shoes
and you will be stunned
and stillborn into the street.

Part Two

The Messenger:

To you, Medea,
I have no more to say.
As for human life,
It is a shadow, as I have long believed.

AFTER MY LITTLE LIGHT, I SAT IN THE DARK

After my little light, I sat in the dark
a long time. The dark was studded with ash
and it had no taste   and it sounded
like the snow of the radio floating
between two stations: my little light
and this dark.

I sat in the dark all night and the morning
reeled up darker than the darkest
closet or cellar   except
now merciful mushrooms (black-capped
and milky in the mouth)
introduced themselves into the world
and their thousand voices clacked the static
like the circle a jump-rope clacks between
two little, white-haired girls.

The night was much darker when it came back
but my eyes were beginning to focus.
And the moss crawled over my shoe
and I saw that in the dark
many things can exist. A worm
sang in the earth like the breath
of a clarinet. Fur

passed my ankle, and I could taste
a murky oyster mold itself out of shadow.

The next day was dark, dark
as the center of a wall of a home
where the termite chews in blindness
and lies but to me
it seemed like twilight. I
was used to this now.
It knew me. I
was familiar among familiar things:

the mice scrambling under
the claws of the owl, the fish
blinking between the slippery stones—
especially the stones who
love nothing who
believe in nothing at all.

When night bled down again, I
had never been happier in my life. My skin
had begun to move
with the pearly eyes of flies
and my hair was sewn up black
and wet, and the black rats bred
and nested peacefully there.

Now I could see that the night
was crowded with others, and their waxy bodies
glistened and lit up the dark. By now
I could see quite well   even
the moldy corners where
the devil smiled.

And he bowed to me as if
I were the queen of all this   supreme
among the others who'd aged here
creeping with snails in the damp. Now
the leeches sang
drunken with my blood,
and the rats began to chew
a hole dead through the center
of the place where once
my little light had been.

The devil knelt to kiss my knees.
We were so pleased to see you, he said,
so young, the adjustment will come
easy to you   and in
the expanding dark I saw
that I was just a girl   a girl
tied to a chair   a girl
in a simple uniform (my mother
had sewn up the hem herself

and the thread danced crooked
across my thighs) I could read
my name on my pocket. He smiled.

He uncurled my legs and spread my knees
and the tongue of the devil was cold
and sharp and the pain
and the shame of it lopped
the top of the dark off.

I was a child. I had homework
to do. My clarinet wept with spit
in its case. The dolls
gasped for breath in the doll house. When
he surfaced again
from between my thighs, still
he smiled (was he kind?
is it possible? was he even shy?)

And I was quiet becoming
one of the devil's many secrets one
of the devil's many toys
so I slid down drowning in dark,
a perfect daughter, an eager student
who had learned to turn
the anguish to pleasure learned
that many things can exist quite pleasantly

in the dark, and when
I opened my eyes I could see:

a girl with no soul   floating
in a flawless uniform   playing
an impeccable clarinet. She
had invented her own self smiling
out of the dark, the dark   as warm
and happy as a home in hell.

MASSACRE OF THE INNOCENTS

after Pieter Brueghel

Pale rubies dripped from the branches
like red gems of ice, and Rachel
was weeping. And the cold
snow of Bethlehem, of Flanders.
The soldiers moved slowly
as a forest, confused
and eager as metal animals. Herod
was sleeping. Rachel
refused to be consoled. Hide
the children, they cried. Hold
the babies higher. But
the world was unraveling. The future
had found them. The pond
was frozen sharp
and white as a wing.
And no one saved them. No. God
fled to Egypt, by donkey
through the snow, cold
snow of Egypt, of Flanders, of France.
A star was seen exploding
in the East, precisely
over themselves. They could have hidden, but

no angel appeared
to them. The soldiers arrived
grey and still, and their mothers
pleaded, and a voice was heard,
too late and wailing. In the cold
snow of Oklahoma,
or Dachau, or Peru. Wailing
and loud lamentation.
An old man got down on his knees
and begged to have
the baby back. Cape
of Good Hope.

THE DEVIL ADDRESSES THE VFW

I decided to decorate the desert with crows
crows, crows and a tree of moons
I was troubled then and always alone
Sometimes I thought I heard
the angels
apologize to me

But now I know that angels
don't apologize for what they do, angels
just dance, fold up
their foil wings and crowd themselves
onto pins
dance their nimbused dances while
comets singe the sky,
toss up metal confetti
like shrapnel, celebrate
the luminous cakewalk of never
having to die

After the party the crows
chew up the dead marines
and all the other
ruined animals, too

I know this because, as you know
I was an angel once myself
but I fell from the sky
with my wings on fire
while the other angels sang about *a cause*

larger than ourselves

But we know their nacreous hands
are never dirty, they never
explode on the earth
with their priggish pajamas aflame

Now I'm alone with my crows
where paratroopers drag
their bellies raw across the world

THE DEVIL EXITS TO CROW SONG:

The first night of wings, we flew.
Fresh out of hell, we nested
there in the tree of moons
because the life-tree
was heavy with lemons
and the tree of death
was milky with angel cocoons.
We shook the tree and the moons
fell next to the mastodon skulls,
scuffed and blasted with sand.

ARMS

On May 5, 1945, a balloon bomb killed five children and a pregnant woman on a church picnic in southern Oregon. As they gathered around the shiny object, it exploded.

Plasma holds the planets
in the sky, and the cross
throws its shadow on the church lawn
as lovely as a naked man, arms
like wings without feathers
open to hold
the ions and electrons
that make us live. The world
is green crystal and spinning.
The youngest girl has
a paper flower in her hair.
They board the bus.

The world should be better, we wonder later.
The pastor's wife might
have had the baby in May. Instead
May explodes like a bride's bouquet
tossed, accidentally,
into a fan.

They are in Oregon. The yellow bus
is safely parked below the slopes. Later
Reverend Archie will sing a prayer
about gathering His children like a hen
gathers her brood beneath her wings
when they are dead. But
this afternoon, he just eats ice cream
and holds the hand
of his wife. There will be shredded petals
and ribbons everywhere, singing
and screaming. The world
will shimmer like a glassy opal.

There's something shiny settling on the mountain.
An animal with no blood. There is
a paper flower in the youngest girl's hair.
In Japan, a thousand cranes
wade in emerald water, tall
and full of wonder, full
of confusion and fear. They float
like paper boats across
the wide, pacific ocean, as calm
as helium this afternoon.
And when the birds hear the echo
of children's singing, eerie
and perfect as a thousand birds,

they explode out of the ocean
in a frenzy of feather and hydrogen.

They fall into the sun
one by one
through the arms of empty air
that open
not to catch us
but to pass us on.

AT THE LAST TRUMPET

after Clifford Brown

Before I died I had wings
of brass and grapes of music
were what I ate. And she
had coiled ropes of hair.
At night I climbed them into
the fantastic skull
of the sky. Naked, music-mad
and leaning into jazz
like the wild milk-fire
of stars.
My body against her body
blindly: Her night black dress
disappeared in the dark, satin,
exploded into blood
of music in her bed.
Like the ceiling torn off the earth.
Like a garden of grapes
tangled in her hair.
I fell down there.
I climbed, she woke.
Every night the lost voice
calling and calling to me

from the sky.
Her breasts like birds, my lungs
like wings of brass.

THE DRIVER'S LULLABY

for Cary, who slept at the wheel

You drive until you pass the place
the sun sets   until you pass the place
the gypsy moths catch fire
and our souls store up like rain

in old cans   and the blue plums turn
to macadam   and the asphalt
blushes   where
the last light makes and snuffs itself.

It is a long drive   flagstone, cobblestone
and the body has its limits. We
are all just weak as flesh in the end
and sleep rouses us   billows us

like bedsheets in the wind   bedsheets
your mother hung in summer.
When you see this again
it is with no sound but cicada hum

or the static rattle of the past:
a burst of cardinal in the lilacs

startles you   and the sky
above you is so blinding

it requires you to be music   and you
are only the size of your arm
in your crib. When your young mother
turns to you   she's holding

fatigue out in her arms   and it's
only a scarf of air   but then
the field turns to black
and barbed wire   and for a moment

you see yourself   in a cow's white eye
driving to sulfur and tin and air
and the hole in the earth where
the soul collects itself. Up ahead

in this night's small town
a barber pole whirls eternal stripes
through the dark   and you
drive past that too.

RADISHES

Love is a wall and hatred is too.
          For instance

          it was afternoon.
The river was white as a river of milk
in the summer glare.

The rockets at the edge of the cornfields crackled.

And I was four,
          half-naked in the garden
          digging radishes with my hands.

My grandmother watched me from the porch, swinging.

          When I had a whole bouquet
          of the roots, raw
          and red already, caked
          with dirt,
          I waved them to her
               and smiled
                    and I laughed.

Because she didn't love me.

Because she had never wanted
a husband, or a daughter,
or even the dream of a grandchild
        abandoned in her backyard,

        she refused the smile.
        She watched me grub
        for that acrid fruit
            with nothing
                on her face.

A sheet of violets
        faded on the clothesline
        whipped the bleached air.

It was the only sound except
for the sound of corn climbing
like that wall.

        Because I knew this even then,
        I stared straight back
        blank at her,
and I began to suck
the dirty radishes, one by one,
        like sour nipples in the sun.

Part Three

The Nurse:

But none of them has discovered
How to put to an end with their poetry
Or musical instruments grief,
Bitter grief, from which death and disaster
Cheat the hopes of a house.

ROSEBUSH

I have dug up my grandfather accidentally
while planting the rosebush behind the shed

His long-buried hair is as gentle and white
as a web, and the spider is silver
and spinning it spinning it
as he rises and says to me: Now
I don't have much time to explain, my dear
so you'll have to make all the arrangements
yourself Be sure to prepare a place
for each of us there

My grandfather speaks to me kindly from death
and the words are so bright they fly
around his head like a shower
of dazzling birds and I am relieved to see
the simple grave
could press all that pain into light like stars
in my own backyard where someday my children
can chip at that grief
with chisels and picks
and shine it and hold it
up to the sun to see the pain plainly in death
as I could never see it in life *Children*

this is the place
where your great-grandfather
turned to ashes of glass   He was a man
who wept bits of glitter
who was never without a drink in his life
and who liked to sip his torment raw

He was a kind man who hated children
but loved a victim and knew
all of the tenderest places to grope
and the wounded for miles knew him
and called him by name

But look   his suffering has turned
to a dust of sparks so fine it startles the eye
The grave must finally suit him
The grave must please him greatly

He says: Now
Be sure there is plenty for everyone there
and don't be afraid   we can be home by Monday
and no one will even know we were gone

I'm delirious with joy as a feverish child
and I see that he is the source
of all music   all the music

my life has made   from him a blinding choir shines
and I finally cry   on my knees
in the dirt   with an armful of thorns   I
am ready to leave with him   anywhere   ready
to take every one of them with me

But when the day comes   (and it does)
I am not so sure   I
am not so sure
I am ready to go

CHRISTMAS SHOPPING

Look at the puppet
who thinks he is alive
in his Christmas boots

who stomps up the hydrogen ice
who stomps up the fiberglass snow, what

incredible loyalty, what
a heavy emptiness
his white shadow
must drag behind him.

This is how my mother looked:
black hair and eyes
so much bluer than mine,
skin whiter, breasts
so much more beautiful.
When they brought me to her,
small and purple as a plum,
she was so lovely she must have thought,
This can't be mine.

Today there are flocks of angels
at the department store

all with bone-meal on their faces
and gauzy dresses blue-white

as her wrist. I
was ten when she told me
there might not be
anything after death.
I argued there had to be.
It was a short lapse of faith
for her. I still believe
in nothing. She

was pale and radiant
as winter on the way.
Luminous, like thin ice.

All those years so beautiful
but she didn't cry
when the cancer cut out her breasts,
when the chemo took her hair.
She said, I'm going to live.
She said I'll be back
when she left.

But I used to spend hours at the mirror
crying about my hair, crying
about my smile, dying
to be beautiful, and not.

She would roll my hair and hug me,
spend fortunes on my teeth
and say, You are, you are.
And still I couldn't be
because I'm not. Now

bisected and my girlhood
melted away like a cup
of pale sherbet, my mother has turned back
into a watery ghost
like she began.
It's December again, the amazing

betrayal of birds
fit enough to fly to Florida
but too weak for winter.
This decline of the sun.
This swamp of snow on the way.
This hilarious memory of my mother
debating faith with a child. *Oh*
what do I know, she told me, *Sweetheart,*
decide for yourself. So

Christmas shopping today, I
start to talk to her the way
other mothers and daughters
talk to each other coldly

over scarves and socks.

I talk without moving my lips the way
I was taught to pray to God

and the same answer blizzards back:

HYMN FROM THE HOUSE OF TROUBLE

So go now my love before you're gone.
Before you're older, sadder, sicker,
gone, though I'll still be
awake and waiting.
I have nowhere else
I want to go.

To go to the door of the House of Trouble
and decide I want to stay
even when they tell me,
There will be three nights of pleasure followed
by thirty years bad luck.
I say, Fine. Let me sleep with that one,
the one the others are afraid of,
the one with the evil twin.

The evil twin with a bottle
who pins my hands behind my back,
whose name is the name of a saint,
a drunken fair-haired angel from hell,
passed out all night like a child in my arms.

There are hymns all night in the House of Trouble,
sacred snapshots of the dead,

sobbing and giggling among the girls,
hysterical, empty cups in the sink.

And all the men are drinkers,
slow drinkers drinking
until they only look like men I love,
until I only love the way they look.

The way he looks, the way he looks.
And the smell of his shirts.
And when his hands, and when his hands.
I'm tangled to death in my own sheets,
gasping and snagged like a trout.

See all these are snapshots of you
looking green-eyed at the beach.
All these snapshots are you before
the bottle in your hand is empty
and all your buddies are maudlin or brawling,
all of you still for a second smiling
like beautiful monsters clapping each other,
sequinned and rising from the great, green lake.

So leave my love because I've become a believer.
And I believe in another God, another life,
a better, harder, longer life to come
and I'll come back and back to this place I am

and when I do it will be with you,
it will be you again.

LOSING SPEED

When it's over I'll say,
There were nice nights.
Some of them taste
like my whole life.
Like the August night
a neighbor paid me
to dance on his picnic table.
The Milky Way smeared
like smoke across the sky.
My mouth open, air
everywhere
and his face lit and floating
on the star of a cigarette.
I was ten and didn't know
I was naked
until now.
Virginity like a memory
of stumbling from the sky,
seeing my soul tumble
from the picnic table to earth,
tossed through my ribs
like a stone without me.
I get older and think of myself
as that thing, dropped

accidentally and forever
into the ocean of the past.
Like the taste of soap
tonight on the Titanic, wine
and cellos
and everyone is beautiful, rich
and sleeping
and you say across a candle,
I want always to be in this bathtub with you.
And I say, Relax.
We're losing speed.
Look how my breasts
have started to sink.

BELLS OF ICE

Nothing is as perfect as gravity.
Even the water would try
to keep us from drowning.
But gravity wants
to bring back winter. Tuesday

is cold as December
in the middle of summer
and every hour they turn her
to keep the skin from fading.
The lake swallows the beach.

Even the water would try, but gravity
turns our existence against us,
turns the weight of being alive
into a burden
of bed sores and trying to die.

A nurse has come again to turn her,
turn her, tumble her
out of her life.

She is plummeting into the tunnel. She
is whirling into the tunnel.

And I can feel the wind, can imagine
the beach today, gasping
in the chill.

I try to hold a snapshot up
for her to see. My dead grandfather's arm
is around her. They
clink glasses some summer.
Cold, beautiful bells of ice
and a picnic table, and a beach.
The lime-gray glasses raised—
A toast!

To anything!
Arbitrary,
our lives are polaroid, so

what is the sense in staying?
The tunnel takes
our memories, too, tortures us later
with our own old snapshots,
our little recollections

of last kisses before deaths.
The tacky statues

we remember

one another with.
All that love and that long stretch of beach
are gone and pitiful
and useless to recall.

We are falling one by one
into its face. The eye of the tunnel
glitters, gaudy and mocking, just
to show us our folly, just
to empty us for the journey.

PORCH

When she died I believed that she was dead, but now
we meet each night in a world between ourselves
where she is more alive
than I have ever been.

On the front porch we talk
and rock in the wicker rockers
that ruined in the rain
even before she was gone.
The dead we love enter
the earth from here:
It is night, the front porch
between a meteor storm
and the new grass growing.

The yard is full of sweet-pea
and poison sumac, bittersweet
and brimstone.
The summer before
and all the summers since

are over and have never been.

In space the stars turn

to ash and incandescence,
but it's too much to try to understand.
She says, Someday you'll learn to see
with all your eyes.

This amazes me.
My breath light is burning down but hers
has turned inward, become
truly lucent,
purely life.
She pulls her nightgown down
to show me the scars again
where they let death out of her.

I turn my head:
too bright, too beautiful.

She laughs. She says,
You're still the weaksister, the one
who was meant to die.

When I wake up
I need to believe—

Though—once I watched a swan die
of a fishhook caught in her throat.
In that still black river

she seemed to sing

but it was pain that peeled
the notes from her.

Maybe that's all it is
to dream about the dead.

PASSION

1

In this stained glass circle Christ
is teaching us to die   with irises
and agony   It proves our human helplessness
and the chaos of our grief becomes
just   a gesture Mary makes   with hands

to her glass breasts   Seen from the sky
we would seem to be   only a mosaic of hats
and rosaries   and wreaths   This
smallness is our triumph   until

we find ourselves later alone   without
the flicker and hymn of candles   breathing
the snow-blue dusk   at 6 p.m. on an ordinary
Michigan night   surrounded by the actual
graves of the actual dead we've loved

Then   only the crystal stars are broken
in the snow   and the ice slips away in chunks
down that cold black stream   Then

it's the other passion that breaks loose
like ice from us   the one that is
the memory of flesh   moving
in the dark   and among the branches
snapping under ice   and this firestorm of snow
the moon's cold heart crawls over us   and we
could stand knee-deep in snow
all night together and burn

2

This is the question created for us: What
can we keep? Tonight the trees are bending
under snow like women beneath the weight
of their hair   and the stars huddle in the sky
as if we'll always be alive   Now

there are no questions left   for his lost bride
For her   the secret is revealed   and we
can't tell her anything else about death

But sometimes I comfort myself by saying to her
Be there when I'm there too   and then
a hand passes me in the dark   just the way
I stood in the kitchen after she died
among her cups and pans   and I thought

I saw her face at the window   I thought
I felt her hand on mine   no different

than the night before her wedding when I took
a cup of wine from her   on a second-story porch
under the sky   and I drank it   and we laughed

It was already so close by then—the kingdom
was enraged that night   with dancing
clapping light   spinning wildly ahead
despite us   We were so close to it
that night   and now I wonder what else there is
that I can't see   in front of me   Now
I understand   completely   that life
and light are free   but we can't keep them

3

I reach across her death to touch
her bridegroom   and I realize
I had forgotten about passion   that
red bird in constant flight
across the frozen field   At night
I can hear moths in the attic   make lace
of my own wedding dress   and I know

if I opened that door now   I could be blinded
in the dark   by deaf white wings   I could watch
my own young husband   who knows
nothing about loss   learn

And when I left those other arms today
I wondered   Could that crushed hand   that
strange gesture   that too bright Christ
of glass and ice be love?   Does he teach us
the comfort of passion too   the movement
of flesh and flesh in the dark: The flash
of a bird in snow?

No   whatever they told us about grief we know
it drinks and lies   and it becomes
a dance of flesh and movement all its own

It lives on beyond us like a bell
that always rings   Even years later
there are nights   that I would rather hold
her wrecked bones than be alone
with this old dream I have that heaven
is howling and unbearable and she can't sleep
and the frantic nurse with her morphine
is invisible in the snow   and we
can't even help each other die

But tonight I'm touching him   and my face
has turned toward   the ruined future
and my hand is at his chest   I want
to think   perhaps it now snows
hopefully outside   while we are still alive
and learning this: That love dies slowly
but it does   and what it leaves behind
looks just like love

Part Four

Medea:

Let the whole house crash.

THE BRIDE BETWEEN THEM

That night his bride's face
becomes the moon's surface
in his bed. Between dreams
he is climbing
the narrow steps to her.
She wakes that night,
saying:

Now, think out
into all that might happen
to us. What it means, the future.
We'll look back later and remember
how it was tonight,
not knowing.

The house fills up with winter
months later. He sweeps up
the fireplace, afraid
to find something
still alive among the ashes.
She is gone, fallen
into the bed of a man
he knows and loves.
Her bridal dress burns black.

Years ago, at any wedding
in any room full of people,
he would not have known
how a man's best friend
could become his bitter enemy,
how the eyes of the woman
he would love would look
moon-cold and closed.

He would not have known
that to crawl up to the black, sad
sleep of love
is not to want to live.
His own ghost glowing there.

In any room full of people
there are already two or three
wearing funeral shrouds
beneath their wedding clothes.
There is one at the altar
who will hold a knife
to the throat of a friend.
A woman who can forget anything.
Two men who might share
the bride between them.

The wind is cold.
Two dark cats claw in the snow.
He stands at the window
and understands
how one sweet creature
could gnaw another to death.

FOLIE À DEUX

The ways of August were mysterious.
The hill sloped warm into the stars
and night-clouds frosted
the low heat, the humid fog
of a gluey moon. Now

our secret madness blooms
like mushrooms, pasty
mushrooms in a ring
where the grass is still pressed flat
from our bodies.
It's August again
and the little, gypsy people who dance
in that place shake
tambourines. It's
a wild dance, and they are drunk.
The hush of faithlessness and lust
means nothing to them. They
screech like nighthawks in their laughter
and smash the prudent rustling
of the hollyhocks this summer, while

worms gore the new apples.
We eat them anyway though

and quickly since they taste
as sour as a blinding light. Now
something strange and full of thorns, moon-
orange and heavy as a warm sleep
grows in that spot. Now
no poison at all can kill
August's gorgeous weed.
Look. Look what we did.

THE SORCERESS AND THE WIFE

She decided she had to have
her neighbor's husband
one summer in the suburb:
in the green
energy of desire, in the heat
lightning of lust.

I asked my friend his wife, Didn't
you ever suspect?
She said, What would I have supposed?
She was our neighbor, our friend, our widow next door.
Black butterflies drifted, amiably,
between our lawns.
Elms lined up like soldiers down the street.
How would I have known
in the ordinary evening, the polite
string quartet of summer, a sorceress
fell in love with my husband?

In the orderly evening, in the beautiful
backyard with a beer
he was an angel asleep in a lawn chair,
one eye closed.

I asked my friend his wife, Weren't you ever, even,
suspicious? No, she told me, how
could I have known then
that my life was a dream I would wake up from?
A moss-green dream, peacock
green, aquamarine and fading.

He was dozing by the sprinkler, his chest
as cool as the skin of a pear and shirtless.

I asked, Wasn't there ever a sign? She tried
to remember but there was only
the early summer evening
a truck of pigs passed the house
on detour off the highway
reeking in the heat, squealing,
peach and silken-fleshed
as a truck of rotten children.

He stretched and sipped from the beer. The buckle
of his bermudas came undone.

OLD WOMEN

My aunt had a furrow filled with rose
water and whale oil on her face.
She dabbed at it with a napkin and ate
her food with her fingers slowly as though
she could even taste
the air around her food.
Her one kept breast hung
like a snout from her. "She's
an old witch," my sister said—hazel-

haired sister who
never lived to turn to leather.

FISH WIFE

He was seasick once while we
stirred the sea greenly with oars.
A net of fish snaked our feet while
he heaved and heaved.
And this is how I know I love the man:

That night there were dippers
of stars in our hair, and fish
on our feet, phosphorescent
and riddled with eggs, each egg dreaming
its mesozoic dream of mud and God
and ooze. The world was already
an ancient forest full
of fossil and creeping possum.
"Damn," he said, "I wish
I wasn't sick."

And I said, "Yes. And fish
wish they had wings."
There was water on his face
and for a moment we were moon-bleached
as I took his hand. The rest of the earth
was empty: We manage with what we have.

That night the strange world
and all our sins slipped into the green. All
his cold shoulders. All
my rages and rants and fish wife lies.
Longing filled my lungs like air
and the wingless fish panted
and my husband heaved into the vast.

Oh, the ocean dredges and ebbs, ebbs
and ebbs and ebbs and dredges.
And one day our teeth will gleam
in the sediment where once we lived
and offered comfort to each other. But

the soul is slippery as a fetus
or a fish. It escapes us in the end, escapes
the world that would destroy it.
And where it goes it cleaves
to what it loves.

EX-WIFE

I miss you now.
The first few years I was busy
unpacking and naming the bats
(some of them hum like pitch pipes
some rattle their teeth in the attic)

and there were the hedges to trim
and peaches in spring
(I ate every one of them green
and sometimes the pain of it
made me scream) but now

the bats don't interest me
and I have let the hedges combust
like wild walls. It makes me
restless to watch the peaches
wither on the trees
like old men's breasts.

TWENTY-NINTH BIRTHDAY

Suddenly I see that I
have been wearing my mother's body
for a long time now. It all
belongs to her, here where the skin
is softest and here
where it puckers in disgust—each
inch. The very nails that pounded
her body to pieces
built me one just like it
and I have been wearing it
like a terrible house
and never noticed—all of it
hers, except this mole on my arm—that
belonged to my father's mother
and it was left to me
to remind me that I
am one of those
witches, too, praying
to the dry face of the moon
while I walk around with death
in my big breasts, like them, full
already of my future scars
and pain and hallucinations
that shriek ahead like train tracks

past this naked house
across the self-pitying
pleasureless decades left.
I have turned my face to the wall to hide it
while you slip my father's
angry face over yours.

COLOMA LANES

When we lived in Coloma we bowled
at Coloma Lanes. In summer the air
was refrigerated there
and the smell of beer was in our shoes.

I was still a girl there
when I heard my step-mother say
to another step-mother:

and how much does a worm suffer anyway?
that's what she is all
she is anyway if
I didn't know her so well
like a sister like
a sister I'd say
she's just a witch like any witch
and deserves whatever she gets

There really were worms bloated
in the twilit parking lot when we left
and the last sun devils of the day
danced around my step-
mother. Her mouth was smooth as a tulip
and she held her purse in both hands

the way an owl
carries a mouse.

Night fell out of the sky while we rode home
from bowling in Coloma
and in the distance the landfill
glowed in the dark.

TO WHOM IT MAY CONCERN,

During the winter   I stayed indoors
and rattled the cups   brained
the tomatoes and canned them   until
the teapot shrieked
and the tea turned brackish
and smelled like bile
and the shoe tree bloomed in the closet   Then
I sent a simple note:

Please   please   marry me
The daisies on the shades are eggish
and bleed   and the pork
reeks on the plate   and I have become a girl
huge and dreadful with love
like a mushroom cloud floating luminous over the lake

Lift me out of this house
as you might lift a child
trapped in the scraps of a car   The edges of this house
are razor sharp
and the collision here has left several dead

I tell you   I
will be limp and simple with pain—

the bed for sex   and the fork for food

Please   marry me   lift me
out of this house
where my father takes my tongue
like a lover   where the family portrait
wails on the wall
where I've danced all winter
among the rubble   clumsy
and pointless on a rug of rags
for the stove   obscene in his gaping
for the toaster's terrible grin

I tell you   I'll be
a guileless wife   rustic
and homely as a farmhouse in snow